IMAGES
of America

BROTHERS OF THE SACRED HEART IN NEW ORLEANS

Starting the Journey. Br. Farrel Lorio, SC, (left, standing) uses an evergreen sprig to bless Br. Barry Landry, SC, who is entering the community as a novice. This ceremony, beautiful in its simplicity, took place at the Brothers of the Sacred Heart novitiate house of formation on City Park Avenue in New Orleans in 1984. Seated behind Brother Farrel (who was also an ordained priest) is Br. Bernard Couvillion, SC, a member of the formation team for the province at the time. (Courtesy of the Brothers of the Sacred Heart, New Orleans.)

On the Cover: The novice class of 1947 is pictured after professing their vows at St. Joseph's House of Studies in Metuchen, New Jersey. The institute (the term the Brothers prefer rather than "Order," which is more appropriate for monastic communities) sent all young men in the United States called to a vocation as a Brother to Metuchen for their novice studies until 1962. (Courtesy of the Brothers of the Sacred Heart, New Orleans.)

IMAGES
of America

Brothers of the Sacred Heart in New Orleans

Edward J. Branley

ARCADIA
PUBLISHING

ISBN 978-0-7385-8567-3

Published by Arcadia Publishing
Charleston, South Carolina

Printed in the United States of America

Library of Congress Control Number: 2009939244

For all general information contact Arcadia Publishing at:
Telephone 843-853-2070
Fax 843-853-0044
E-mail sales@arcadiapublishing.com
For customer service and orders:
Toll-Free 1-888-313-2665

Visit us on the Internet at www.arcadiapublishing.com

This book is dedicated to the Brothers, lay faculty, and staff of Brother Martin High School from the 2005–2006 school year, led by Pres. John Devlin and Principal Gene Tullier.

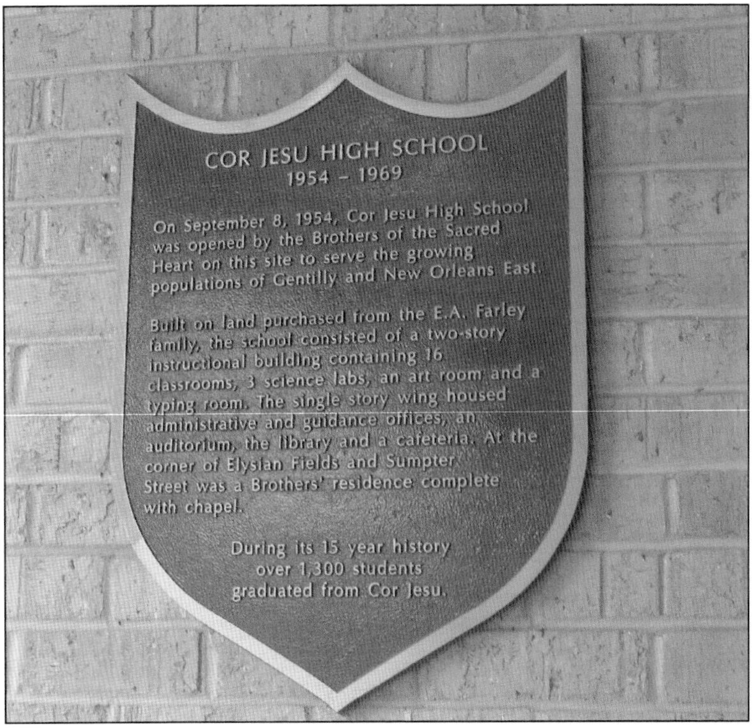

Cor Jesu. This is the plaque on the wall of the original classroom building of Cor Jesu High School. Brother Martin High School (BMHS) students now refer to this as the "old building." Cor Jesu was, in so many ways, totally absorbed into BMHS when the school was merged with St. Aloysius High in 1969. This plaque is a reminder of the first Brothers school in Gentilly. (Courtesy of the Brothers of the Sacred Heart, New Orleans.)

Contents

FOREWORD

As a Brother of the Sacred Heart and a native of New Orleans, I am very grateful to Edward Branley for undertaking the task of chronicling through photographs the constant commitment and dedication that the Brothers have shown to the youth of the New Orleans area. Like Edward, I was educated by the Brothers of the Sacred Heart. We obviously were both inspired by the Brothers. I completed St. Aloysius in 1965, and Edward finished Brother Martin High School in 1976. The Brothers had such a profound and positive impact on me that I chose to join ranks with them in an effort to emulate their good works. Through his telling of the story of a long and loving relationship between the Brothers and the New Orleans community, I believe Edward shares deep insights into the many intangible ways that the spirit of the Brothers of the Sacred Heart has touched his life and the lives of many New Orleans youth.

The Preamble to the *Rule of Life* of the Brothers defines the purpose of the founding of our institute with these words: "To rescue young people from ignorance, to prepare them for life, and to give them a knowledge and love of religion, Father Andre Coindre, in 1821, founded the Institute of the Brothers of the Sacred Heart." Since 1821, the Brothers have committed themselves to live out this founding inspiration of Father Coindre. Over the 140 years that the Brothers have been in New Orleans, this basic educational mission has been articulated through the words, actions, and lives of hundreds of Brothers to thousands of students.

To achieve the goals of our founding, the Brothers have utilized a threefold approach to education: instruction, formation, and witness. They have always understood that good instruction is essential to provide the skills and knowledge needed for an individual to become the full person that God intends him or her to be. Equally important has been the original mandate to "prepare them for life." Thus, the Brothers have given great emphasis to the personal formation of students to positive attitudes, Christian values, and healthy core beliefs, which provide the essential foundation for a moral and happy life. Most importantly, the witness of the Brothers to a life dedicated to learning, rooted in faith, and motivated by love has offered hope, support, and encouragement to youth who daily deal with the complexity of the adolescent years. My hope is that the pictures in this book enable you to see this witness and to experience the depth of love and faith that the Brothers have brought to their work.

What the Brothers have taught and how they have taught has changed over the years. Our first brothers in France taught silk weaving. In the early days of the Brothers in New Orleans, there was strong emphasis on commercial subjects like typewriting, shorthand, and bookkeeping. Today the emphasis is on college preparatory courses. Yet what has remained constant through the changing times is that what is taught is not nearly as important as the person being taught. This quote in the lobby of Brother Martin High School speaks to this belief: "We are not here to teach boys how to make a living, but how to make a life." These 1949 words of Br. Martin Hernandez to the graduating seniors of St. Aloysius emphasize the Brothers' concern for development of the individual into a person prepared to live life fully. *Educational Mission and Ministry*, a document currently being used in the direction of our schools, articulates the importance of the person understanding his or her own goodness and worth with these words: "We see our schools as successful if students graduate with a strong belief that God loves them."

Rule 151 of the Brothers' *Rule of Life* states, "It is not sufficient just to instruct our students; we must also afford them a formation which enables them to improve the earthly city by furthering the reign of Christ." New Orleans is the earthly city where the Brothers have toiled for 140 years. Our goal has been to improve this earthly city through well-educated, highly principled, and faith-filled young people who have learned from the instruction, formation, and witness of the Brothers and their lay partners in education.

For those of you who have been a part of the Brothers of the Sacred Heart history in New Orleans, I hope that this book is an opportunity to relive some of the experiences and relationships that have helped you to grow to the person you are today. For those of you less familiar with the Brothers, I hope this book illustrates the good that can be achieved when individuals are willing to sacrifice self-interest and to work together. My prayer is that this book may serve as an inspiration to all who read it, an inspiration that compels them to work to build up this earthly city of New Orleans by promoting the common good, maintaining harmonious relations, and acting with good intentions.

Through this book, Edward Branley has done a great service for the Brothers of the Sacred Heart. Not only does he give us a pictorial history; he calls us to a renewed emphasis on those values and those principles that transcend time and place and have their roots in the Gospels, in the inspiration of our founding in Lyon, France, and in our initial work here in New Orleans. Thank you, Edward, for recalling so well the Brothers' mission of instruction, formation, and witness and for giving it life here on these pages.

—Br. Ronald Talbot, SC, (St. Aloysius class of 1965) Provincial
Brothers of the Sacred Heart,
New Orleans Province

Acknowledgments

Thanks to Amy Perryman, my editor at Arcadia, for believing in the project from the start. My deepest gratitude goes to everyone in the BOSH/BMHS community for their assistance and support, particularly Tommy Mitchell (class of 1979), assistant to the president and director of development; Kenny Spellman (class of 1984), alumni director; and Dennis Panepinto (class of 1981), events director/webmaster. My appreciation and respect go to all of the Brothers who assisted me. Thanks to Greg Rando (class of 1977), principal of BMHS, and Br. Francis David, SC, for liking the idea of the book in the first place and to Br. Ronald Talbot, SC, (St. Aloysius class of 1965) the current provincial in New Orleans, for graciously contributing the book's foreword. Br. Bernard Couvillion, SC, offered wonderful insight on the Rule of Life (as well as resuming his role as my Composition II teacher). Br. Neal Golden, SC, (Cor Jesu class of 1957) provided a wealth of knowledge on the sports history of the schools, as well as many other aspects of the institute's history. Br. Henry Gaither, SC, and Br. Ivy LeBlanc, SC, were extremely helpful with factual points in the copy and photograph identifications. Thanks to Dominick Caronna (class of 1985), assistant band director, for finding some wonderful band photographs. Also thanks to Maj. Lester Amick, USMC (Retired), and Barry Hebert (class of 1974), BMHS athletic director, for photograph identification help.

All my love goes to my wife, Helen, and my sons, Justin (class of 2006) and Kevin (class of 2012), for putting up with me during the project. A huge thank-you goes to Jenifer Hill Akers for her copyediting skills. Thanks to the Special Collections staff at the Earl K. Long Library, University of New Orleans; Sally Stassi at the Historic New Orleans Collection; and Kara Brockman of the Archives Division, Clerk of Civil District Court, City of New Orleans. Irene Wainwright, archivist, Louisiana Collection, New Orleans Public Library, and her staff were wonderful to work with once again. Thanks to Arthur Hardy, Danny Ford (creator and webmaster of the BMHS Baseball Fan Web site), and Jack Dever for their photographs. Special thanks to the folks at the PJ's Coffee Shop in Clearview Mall for giving me a wonderful work environment to escape to.

A Note on Abbreviations: The Brothers of the Sacred Heart (BOSH) Alumni Association uses three notations to indicate the year a man graduated from one of the three schools: (SA 1965) indicates a St. Aloysius grad, (CJ 1957) one from Cor Jesu, and just the year of graduation (2009) indicates Brother Martin High. Additionally, to make the distinction between Br. Martin Hernandez, SC, and the school named in his honor, Brother Martin High School is referred to by the abbreviation BMHS.

Photograph Credits: Unless otherwise noted, photographs in this book are courtesy of the Brothers of the Sacred Heart, New Orleans Province, and Brother Martin High School.

INTRODUCTION

It's all about the neighborhoods. To understand the contribution the Brothers of the Sacred Heart have made to New Orleans, one must understand the neighborhoods they have served for over 140 years. The institute was founded in 1821, in Lyons, France, by Abbé André Coindre. The Brothers brought their mission of educating young people to America in 1847, opening a school in Mobile.

The Brothers came to New Orleans from the east, via a route similar to the one the British took in 1814. Unlike the British, they were well received, moving from Mobile to Bay St. Louis, Mississippi, opening St. Stanislaus College in 1854. St. Stanislaus accepted local students as well as boarders, but the Civil War forced the Brothers to close the school to boarders. A temporary school was opened in New Orleans in Faubourg Marigny (Annunciation Church Parish).

New Orleans was relatively untouched by the war and began to grow as soon as peace settled upon the country. Archbishop John Mary Odin invited the institute to establish a presence in the city. The Brothers purchased a building on Barracks and Chartres Streets, opening St. Aloysius Academy in 1869. Six students enrolled when the doors were opened, becoming 60 by the end of that first term and growing to 125 students by 1875.

Large numbers of Italian immigrants settled in the French Quarter in the 1880s. The Brothers rose to the challenge of educating the young men of these families, expanding the campus by buying an adjacent house. By 1892, these two buildings could not handle the enrollment. Taking advantage of the moves of other religious groups away from the French Quarter, the Brothers purchased a building located at the corner of Esplanade Avenue and North Rampart Street. This property had been developed by the Ursuline Sisters, who were shifting their focus to the Uptown neighborhood. Br. Justin Roche, SC, supervised the move to Faubourg Marigny. "The Marigny" is the neighborhood just downriver from the Quarter. These neighborhoods would be the home base of the institute until 1969. An outbreak of yellow fever in the summer of 1905 reduced enrollment that September to 75 boys, but that number rose steadily once the epidemic passed.

The Brothers had their first experience with a major hurricane in 1915. A storm hit the city on September 29 of that year, badly damaging St. Aloysius. The Brothers quickly recovered, returning to regular operations and enrolling a record 225 boys by the end of the 1915 term.

The Brothers continued to acquire property around Esplanade and North Rampart throughout the post–World War I years. The rapid growth of Faubourg Marigny, Bywater, and the Ninth Ward prompted the city to expand North Rampart Street from Esplanade Avenue, continuing downriver. To widen the intersection in 1924, the city expropriated land at the corner, forcing the Brothers to tear down the building they had purchased in 1892. The city paid them $40,000 for the expropriated property. The Brothers borrowed $100,000 and began construction in the summer of 1925.

St. Aloysius continued to increase enrollment, becoming the largest private school in the city. Under the leadership of principal Br. Martin Hernandez, SC, St. Aloysius changed its colors from purple and gold to crimson and white to eliminate confusion with Warren Easton. Brother Martin also changed the school's mascot from the Panthers to the Crusaders.

Under the direction of Br. Martinian Pauc, SC, the New Orleans Province continued to serve the French Quarter and Faubourg Marigny at St. Aloysius through the World War II years. Noting the growth of the city north from old Creole neighborhoods out to Milneburg by Lake Pontchartrain, the Brothers made the decision to acquire 7 acres of land along Elysian Fields Avenue near Gentilly Road from Elmer A. Farley. They built a two-story classroom building with an adjacent administrative wing and a large residence for the Brothers. On September 8, 1954, Cor Jesu High School opened its doors. The presence of the Brothers of the Sacred Heart now reached from the Quarter through Faubourg Marigny, into Bywater and the Ninth Ward, north to Faubourg St. John into Gentilly, and into New Orleans East.

The 1960s brought a marked shift in demographics in the older neighborhoods. Younger generations of the immigrants that dominated the Quarter from 1880 to 1930 were moving to Lakeview and Gentilly. The combination of cheap property and "white flight" motivated many to leave the city altogether, moving to suburban parishes. As the end of the decade approached, it became clear to the Brothers that there was a need to shift focus from the older neighborhoods to the newer. The now-40-year-old St. Aloysius campus was in need of major repairs and upgrades, forcing the New Orleans Province to contemplate whether such an investment would be prudent. The decision was made to invest in Gentilly; Cor Jesu would be expanded and St. Aloysius would be closed.

The decision to consolidate operations on Elysian Fields Avenue left the Brothers with a unique challenge. Closing St. Aloysius would mean abandoning a century of tradition and history in favor of a school that was only 15 years old. To smooth over the transition, the Brothers essentially closed both schools, merging the history and traditions formed on both campuses into a new entity. The Gentilly campus grew, with a two-story classroom wing and student center/cafeteria added.

The New Orleans Province decided to name the new, combined school after one of their own, Br. Martin Hernandez, SC. Br. Mark Thornton, SC, was named the school's first principal. Brother Mark's administrative skills and personality were significant contributions to a successful transition. The new school adopted Cor Jesu's colors (crimson and gold) and alma mater and St. Aloysius's mascot (Crusaders) and fight song.

The combination of two of the largest boys' prep schools in New Orleans gave Brother Martin High a dominating athletics program. BMHS basketball teams won back-to-back state championships, and the Crusader football team brought home the state trophy in the 1971–1972 season. The excitement generated by these victories went a long way toward unifying the student body. BMHS continued the Naval Junior Reserve Officer's Training Corps (NJROTC) unit activated at St. Aloysius in 1967.

The story of the second century of service to New Orleans by the Brothers of the Sacred Heart was one of unparalleled growth through the new millennium. That growth was dealt a severe blow on August 29, 2005, when floodwaters pushed into the city by Hurricane Katrina burst barriers on the London Avenue and Industrial Canals. Gentilly was flooded with as much as 12 feet of water. Perched high on the Gentilly Ridge, Brother Martin High received between 1 and 2 feet of water, which was enough to do significant damage. The storm's impact forced the faculty and student body to scatter. The Brothers and lay staff immediately went into action. While teams began repairs in Gentilly, the Brothers restructured operations at their school in Baton Rouge, Catholic High, to allow Brother Martin students to attend classes in the evenings. Three weeks to the day after the storm, Brother Martin–Baton Rouge opened, continuing the fall 2005 semester. Repair work continued, and the Gentilly campus reopened for the second semester of the 2005–2006 school year in January.

With a smaller post-storm student body, the work of the Brothers of the Sacred Heart in New Orleans continues to move forward. The school will renew the full junior high program operated at St. Aloysius by expanding to seventh grade in the 2009–2010 school year.

Even though their numbers have decreased in recent years, the charism of the Brothers of the Sacred Heart, that gift from the Holy Spirit that makes the institute what it is, remains strong, touching students through the remaining Brothers as well as the committed laity working with them.

One

Origins

Brother Polycarp, Brother Xavier, and our other predecessors followed in the footsteps of our founder, in gentleness and humility, growing in sanctity as they lived out our motto and shared hope—Ametur Cor Jesu!

—Article 12, *The Rule of Life of the Brothers of the Sacred Heart* (2007)

In 1869, the institute acquired a two-story building on the corner of Barracks and Chartres Streets, and it opened St. Aloysius Academy that September. The first floor was converted into three classrooms. The second floor was built with a parlor, community room, and chapel, and the five Brothers who staffed the school slept in the attic. By 1884, the building was just too crowded, and Br. Arnould Bererd, SC, and the staff purchased the house next door.

In 1892, the Ursuline Sisters decided to leave Faubourg Marigny, focusing their work at their school on State Street, Uptown. The Sisters sold their building on the corner of Esplanade Avenue and North Rampart Street to the Brothers, who moved in for the fall term.

Br. Cyprian Sanhet, SC, became principal in 1902, supervising the school during a yellow fever epidemic in 1905. Enrollment dropped sharply because of that outbreak. Br. Alphonse Journy, SC, became principal that year, and St. Aloysius's enrollment blossomed in his 11-year tenure. The school and staff weathered the severe damage caused by the Hurricane of 1915, and enrollment continued to grow once repairs were completed. The Brothers purchased most of the block at Esplanade and North Rampart in the post–World War I period.

The neighborhoods of Faubourg Marigny and Bywater continued to grow after World War I, and the city desired to widen North Rampart Street to allow for two-track streetcar operations in the neutral ground. The city used its power of eminent domain to expropriate a portion of the corner of Esplanade and North Rampart, forcing the Brothers to demolish the Ursuline building.

Abbé Coindre. This painting, captioned, "Father Andre Coindre, joyfully giving his Brothers of the Sacred Heart charge of the education of youth," is by an unknown artist (probably done in the 1820s).

The Institute's Founder. Abbé André Coindre founded the Brothers of the Sacred Heart in 1821 in Lyons, France. Coindre died in 1826, and his brother, Vincent, assumed leadership of the institute until 1841, when Brother Polycarp was the first brother named superior general.

Bay St. Louis. A grave marker in the cemetery at St. Stanislaus College (SSC) in Bay St. Louis, Mississippi, marks the passing of several of the Brothers who first came to America.

St. Aloysius Academy. This architectural drawing depicts the building located at the corner of Barracks and Chartres Street in the French Quarter at the time of its purchase by the institute in 1869. Prior to photography, sales of property in New Orleans would be accompanied by a "plan book plan," which usually included a description of the property, a map of the city block in which it was located, and an artist's illustration of the building(s). The building was originally built as officers' quarters for the Spanish garrison of the city. This is the only known illustration of the "first St. Aloysius." (Courtesy of the Archives Division, Clerk of Civil District Court, City of New Orleans.)

Robinson Atlas. This 1880 atlas shows the location of St. Aloysius Academy in Block 18. Just to the left, in Block 19, is the archbishop's residence and St. Mary's Church. The residence is now known as the Old Ursuline Convent. The church, which has had several names, is currently called St. Mary's Italian Church. (Courtesy of the Archives Division, Clerk of Civil District Court, City of New Orleans.)

Barracks and Chartres Streets. This photograph is of the building currently on this corner of the French Quarter, which is Le Richelieu Hotel. (Author's collection.)

Lagarde's Champions. This shot of the 1910 basketball team is the earliest photograph of a St. Aloysius sports team: from left to right are (seated) Roger Neyrey, Marion LeBlanc, Walter Bernissant, and Henry Lagarde; (standing) Louis Romaguera, Rene Garrot, Ernest Lagarde, and Manuel Borneo.

Br. Stanislaus Keating, SC. Born on October 2, 1843, in Tipperary, Ireland, Brother Stanislaus was St. Aloysius College's first director. He held that position until 1875. Brother Stanislaus died in 1932 at the age of 88, having served the institute for 73 years.

THE SECOND SCHOOL. St. Aloysius moved from Barracks and Chartres Streets to the corner of Esplanade Avenue and North Rampart Street in 1892. The Ursuline Sisters sold the Brothers their school building at that location. This photograph was published in a book dated 1903, but the image dates from 1893–1894. Street railway electrification began in New Orleans in 1895, and there are no overhead wires at the corner in this photograph. (Courtesy of the Louisiana Collection, New Orleans Public Library.)

CLASS OF 1923. Here is a charming photograph of the graduates from 1923. From left to right are (seated) Sheldon Hannemann, Pierre Archinard (who was also captain of the football team), Marion Lanasa, and Robert Saucier; (standing) Clarence Reine, Malcom Joanen, James Terrell, Phillip Bayon, Carroll Granger, and Esler D'Aquin. By the 1960s, St. Aloysius was graduating over 200 young men a year.

"STERN TASKMASTERS." At least that is what the *Clarion Herald* newspaper said of the 1910 St. Aloysius faculty. The teachers were all Brothers of the Sacred Heart. From left to right are (seated) Brothers Anthony Cournut, Artus Besset, Alphonse Journy, and Paul Couffort; (standing) Brothers Bonaventure Kenny, John Faure, Adelard Santerre, Austin Rogues, and Rodriguez Soleliac. Brother Alphonse, SC, was the principal.

Esplanade. For this view of Esplanade Avenue from around 1915–1920, the photographer is standing on Esplanade, just on the lake side of the North Rampart Street intersection. The live oaks along the neutral ground have their trunks painted white to discourage termites.

Lower Grades. Here are the lower-grade classes in 1923. St. Aloysius College enrolled elementary school students in the 1920s. The Brothers kept the seventh grade until World War II.

TURN-OF-THE-CENTURY NEW ORLEANS. St. Aloysius was at Esplanade Avenue, the eastern side of the French Quarter; Canal Street was the western boundary of the neighborhood. The northern boundary was Rampart Street, which got its name because there actually was a wall around the early city. Although Canal Street never had a canal, one was originally planned, which is the reason it is such a wide street. This photograph of Canal and North Rampart Streets from 1915 shows the constant hustle-bustle of the Central Business District as all the streetcar lines come together. From where the photographer is standing, St. Aloysius was a 14-block walk to the left. (Courtesy of the Louisiana State Museum.)

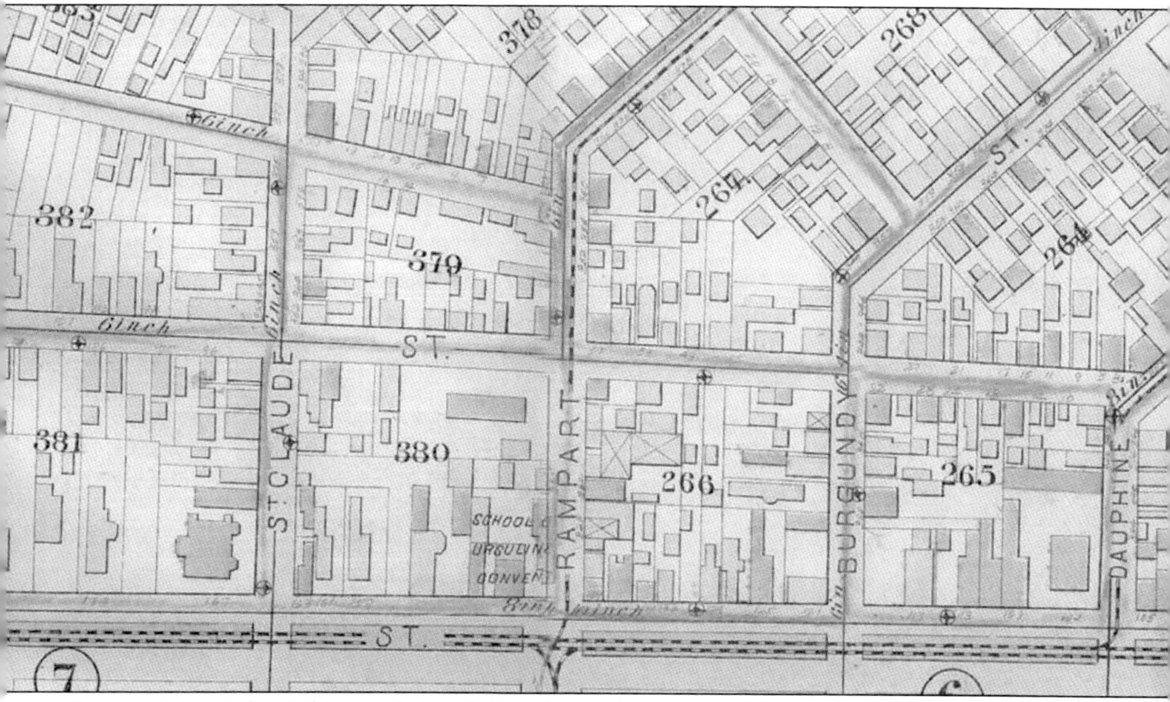

Transit Hub. The Robinson Atlas of 1880 shows the corner of Esplanade Avenue and North Rampart Street. The Ursuline school is visible in the bottom right corner of block 380. Streetcars on the St. Claude line, running down North Rampart, operated in a single-track configuration. Streetcars running on Esplanade Avenue would turn right at North Rampart and head into the Central Business District. In 1924, the city planned to widen North Rampart to permit two-track streetcar operation in the neutral ground. This decision required the Brothers to tear down the Ursuline building. (Courtesy of the Archives Division, Clerk of Civil District Court, City of New Orleans.)

"BONNY." Br. Bonaventure Kenny, SC, and the 1917 basketball team are pictured here. The stripe on these uniforms was purple, and the "A" was in gold, those being the school's colors in this period. Brother Bonaventure served in numerous capacities at St. Aloysius and was the bookstore manager when the school closed in 1969.

Two

Esplanade and North Rampart

The brothers take part in the mission of the Church by the witness of their lives and by their dedication to Christian education, especially that of young people.

—Article 18, *The Rule of Life of the Brothers of the Sacred Heart* (2007)

The City of New Orleans used the power of eminent domain to expropriate property owned by the institute at the corner of Esplanade Avenue and North Rampart Street so that Rampart could be widened. The old Ursuline School, however, was so close to the existing street that the building would have to be torn down. The Brothers had acquired most of the block between North Rampart and St. Claude Avenue, so plans were made to build a new, expanded facility. Construction began at the end of the spring semester in 1925, and the "third" St. Aloysius College opened in September of that year.

St. Aloysius College continued to grow through the late 1920s and early 1930s at an exciting rate. In 1935, Br. Martin Hernandez, SC, became principal, a position he held for 14 years. An excellent administrator who was well loved by the students, Brother Martin made a number of changes in his first years. Brother Martin guided the school through the Great Depression and the war years with an eye on what the future would bring.

THE NEW BUILDING. This Franck Studios photograph is possibly the oldest photograph of the 1925 St. Aloysius school building. The street-widening project that motivated the city to expropriate land from the Brothers is visible on the right. The gym building was built around the corner, facing Kerlerec Street. (Courtesy of the Historic New Orleans Collection.)

Graduates. This is a composite photograph of the senior class of 1928.

Freshmen. The handwritten notation on this photograph describes these boys as the "1st Class" of 1937–1938, what we would call "freshmen" today.

Tennis, Anyone? The 1933 tennis team consisted, from left to right, of L. Choppin, G. Ulrich, Richard Mestayer, Frank Schaeffer, and Francis Reso. Br. Finian Howe, SC, (not pictured) was their coach.

Class Photograph. Here is another class photograph from the 1930s. The specific class is unknown.

Streetcars. Above is a Tenussion Studios photograph of Perley A. Thomas streetcar No. 828, running on the St. Claude line. Below, the corner of Esplanade Avenue and North Rampart Street in front of St. Aloysius was the end of the St. Claude line; the Canal and Esplanade Belt lines operated on the other side of North Rampart Street. (Both courtesy of the NOPSI Collection, Earl K. Long Library, University of New Orleans.)

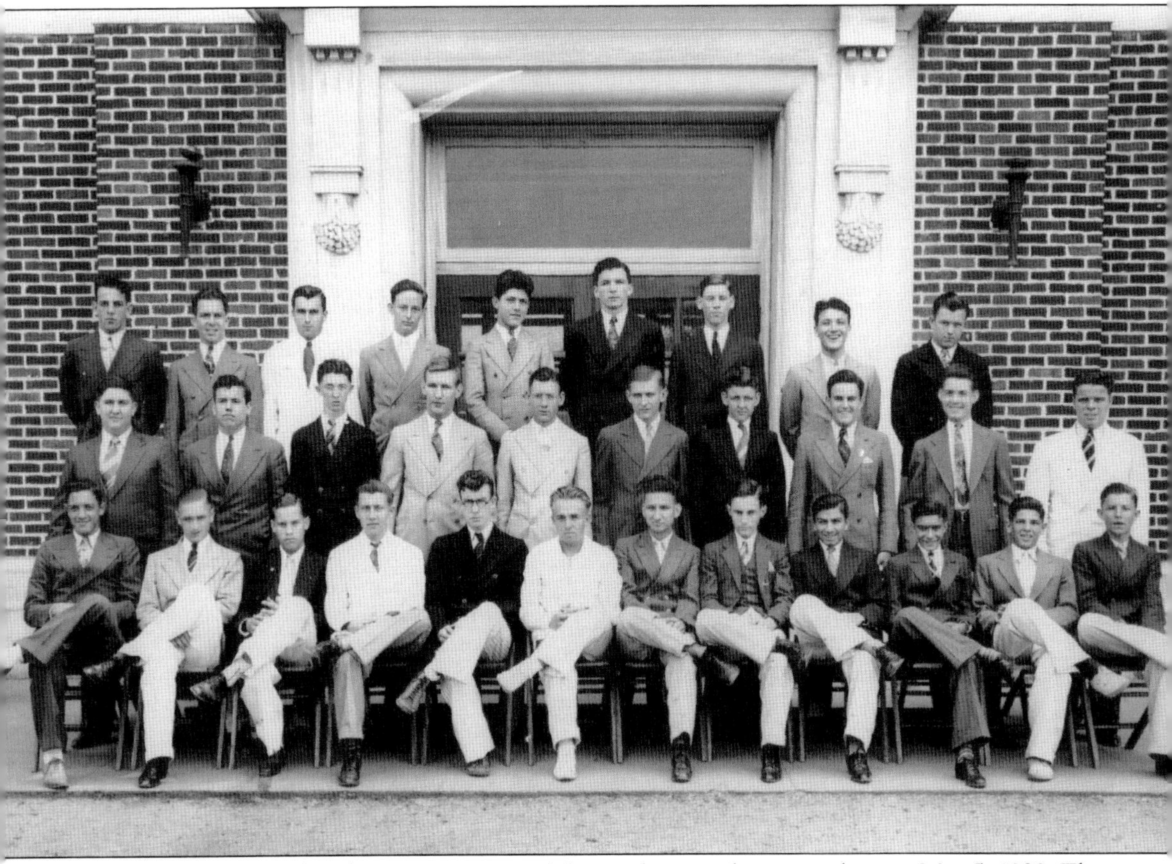

Class of 1938. This charming portrait of the graduating class was taken on May 5, 1938. The name of Brother Bonaventure, SC, is handwritten across the top, but it is not clear why.

THE GYM. The gym at St. Aloysius was built in the 1930s. In addition to physical education classes and sports games/practices, the gym's mezzanine, in the background, was used for typing classes.

Devotion and Good Works. The Sodalities at St. Aloysius were student organizations whose focus was helping dedicated young men grow in the Catholic faith while performing several of the Corporal Works of Mercy (most notably feeding the hungry). Officers for the Senior Sodality for the 1932–1933 school year were, from left to right, (seated) J. David; G. Knobloch; Br. Anselm McGuire, SC, the moderator; A. Richard; and R. Wegmann; (standing behind the seniors, the junior classmen who took over for them at the end of the year) O. Stein, H. Flack, and two unidentified students.

Tad Gormley Stadium. One of the most visible WPA projects constructed in the city during the Great Depression was a horseshoe-shaped stadium built in 1937. The stadium, named for Frank "Tad" Gormley, is the home stadium for the teams of the Catholic League athletic district. This photograph is from the 1941 St. Aloysius–Holy Cross football game on November 6, 1941. (Courtesy of the Louisiana Collection, New Orleans Public Library.)

Brother Ralph. Br. Ralph McGarry, SC, served as head basketball coach at St. Aloysius from 1941 to 1945. Brother Ralph also served as coach Harry "Wop" Glover's assistant for football, assuming head coach duties for the last game of the 1942 season as Glover left the school to join the navy. Brother Ralph prepared the team for the 1943 season until Br. Martin Hernandez, SC, hired Roy "Chief" Ary to lead the Crusaders. Brother Ralph also coached the baseball team in 1941.

Homeroom, 1937. This dapper group of young men and their teacher, an unidentified Brother, were a class from the 1937 school term.

INSIDE THE FENCE. Another Franck photograph shows St. Aloysius in the late 1920s. The extensive front yard served through the years as anything from a recreational area to a parade ground for the NJROTC unit in the 1960s. (Courtesy of the Historic New Orleans Collection.)

CHEERLEADERS. The 1946 cheerleading squad pauses for a photograph during a football game at Tad Gormley Stadium. The cheerleaders were all male at this time.

FORWARD-LOOKING. Br. Martinian Pauc, SC, managed the New Orleans Province in the 1940s. Brother Martinian made the acquisition of the Gentilly property that would become Cor Jesu High in the 1950s.

Marching Band. Pictured is the 1946 band. Note the name of the school on the bass drum. "St. Aloysius High School" has replaced "St. Aloysius College."

"Prof." Joseph Taverna was band director at St. Aloysius from the 1940s to the 1960s. The band room in the Ridgely Fine Arts Center at BMHS is named in his honor.

Relaxing at St. Stanislaus. Br. Marion McCarley, SC, is shown relaxing at St. Stanislaus in this undated photograph from the late 1930s.

Freshmen Class. Br. Cyr Balaney, SC, poses with his freshman homeroom from 1948.

THE MAIN GATE. This illustration of the main gate at St. Aloysius dates from the late 1930s.

SECOND BASEBALL TEAM. What we now call the junior varsity was referred to as the "second" team in the 1930s. The two different uniform styles was typical; some players were on both first and second teams, so they wore the first team uniform (with just the "A"). This was the 1930 "second" team, from left to right: (first row) James Brennan and Robert Craven; (second row) Norman Martina, Joseph Chapron, Joseph Gemelli, Maurice Olivier, and Jorda Elliot; (third row) Coach Siragusa, Eddie Noullet, Philip Blanke, Clarke Cosse, unidentified, and Charles Schaefer.

Formal Portraits. At right, Br. Louis Cavell, SC, poses for a formal portrait. Below, Brother Louis again is pictured with his sister, Sister Leo, a Marianite of Holy Cross, and his mother, Ernestine Whitmore Cavell. Having children enter the religious life was a source of pride for many Catholic families. In 1949, the consul of France in New Orleans conferred on Brother Louis the award of *Palms Academiques* for his contributions to the advancement of the French language in Louisiana.

North Rampart Street and Esplanade Avenue. This is the side of the St. Aloysius school building viewed from North Rampart Street. Rampart Street is a major thoroughfare in New Orleans, linking the downtown and uptown sides of the city.

On the Road. From left to right, Brothers Roy Reinecke, Camille Braud, Claude Petrus, and Clement Cosgrove are in Baton Rouge in 1937.

BROTHERS' RESIDENCE. This Creole mansion at 1137 Esplanade Avenue served as the main residence for the Brothers working at St. Aloysius and at other locations in the city. As it was often overcrowded, some Brothers would sleep in a dormitory in the attic.

NICK REVON. Arguably the best athlete to ever attend St. Aloysius, Nick Revon (no. 13 on the right) poses with teammates in 1946. In his 1944–1948 career at St. Aloysius, Revon earned four letters in basketball, four in baseball, three in track, and two in football. Revon went on to success as a college and semipro basketball player, eventually returning to coach basketball at St. Aloysius. He then moved on and coached for decades at East Jefferson High School in Metairie. With Revon in this photograph are George Vila (no. 10) and John Cronin (no. 5). These players made both the All-City and All-State teams for the 1945–1946 season.

CAMP STANISLAUS. Many New Orleans families would send their boys to summer camp at St. Stanislaus in the 1940s and 1950s. The school's location on Bay St. Louis generated all sorts of potential for keeping boys busy during the days, and the cool evening breeze coming in from the bay was much more enjoyable than hot (and most likely non-air-conditioned) New Orleans nights.

METUCHEN. Novices are shown making profession at mass in the chapel at St. Joseph's House of Studies in Metuchen, New Jersey, in the late 1940s.

ARCHBISHOPS' RESIDENCE. The Wright-Slocomb House was located at 1205 Esplanade Avenue, across Kerlerec Street from St. Aloysius. Originally a private residence, this mansion became the residence of Archbishops Placide Chapelle, James Blenk, and John Shaw. In 1955, Rev. John F. Basty, pastor of St. Augustine Parish, purchased the mansion for $65,000. He offered the house to St. Aloysius, asking that, in return, the Brothers offer reduced tuition for boys living in his parish. The mansion was renamed Basty Hall, and it provided much-needed classroom space. The chancery offices became the office and residence for the provincial superior of the Brothers' U.S. province.

MEANWHILE, OUT IN GENTILLY . . . The corner of Elysian Fields Avenue and Gentilly Road is pictured in 1937. This photograph was shot prior to the WPA work done in the neighborhood to pave and improve roads. By this time, the "Smokey Mary" railroad to Milneburg has been discontinued, and there was no serious automobile access to the lakefront. Hebrew Rest Cemetery is visible on the left side of the street. The land on the right-hand side would become Cor Jesu High. (Courtesy of the Louisiana Collection, New Orleans Public Library.)

Paving Gentilly Road. The Works Progress Administration, the first big "economic stimulus" package implemented in the United States, included street improvement projects all across New Orleans. The neighborhood has grown since the picture above. (Courtesy of the Louisiana Collection, New Orleans Public Library.)

Cor Jesu Drive. Mandeville Street, looking north from Gentilly Road, was also paved as part of the WPA project. Elysian Fields Avenue is just out of the photograph to the left. The empty land in that city block is now a cluster of small buildings and a (now closed) fire station. The land to the right of Mandeville Street eventually became E. A. Farley Florist and Nursery and is now E. A. Farley Field, the baseball diamond and athletic fields for BMHS. In 1994, this block of Mandeville Street was renamed Cor Jesu Drive to commemorate the school. (Courtesy of the New Orleans Public Library.)

COLLEGE RUN. Br. Martin Hernandez, SC, (kneeling, far right) and Br. Ralph McGarry, SC, (standing, far right) escort a group of St. Aloysius students on a campus visit to the University of Mississippi in the early 1950s.

COOL CAR! Br. Louis Cavell, SC, poses next to his mother's Cadillac. Brother Louis was active with student dramatic and musical productions as well as the moderator of the band at St. Aloysius in the 1940s.

BANDSMEN. This portrait of two bandsmen from 1946 shows the military-style uniform of the period, complete with "Sam Browne" pistol belts.

Keeping Busy. Camp Stanislaus counselors move boys from one activity to another. The more they kept them busy, the better they slept at night. The camp presented a tough challenge for Brother Martin, SC, as provincial. It was a moneymaker for SSC but required Brothers to remain at the bay for the summer as staff. Many of the Brothers wanted to attend university classes during their summer break.

Lunch Break. Here are students hanging out in the school's yard at St. Aloysius in the 1930s. The yard faced Esplanade Avenue, and North Rampart Street is in the background.

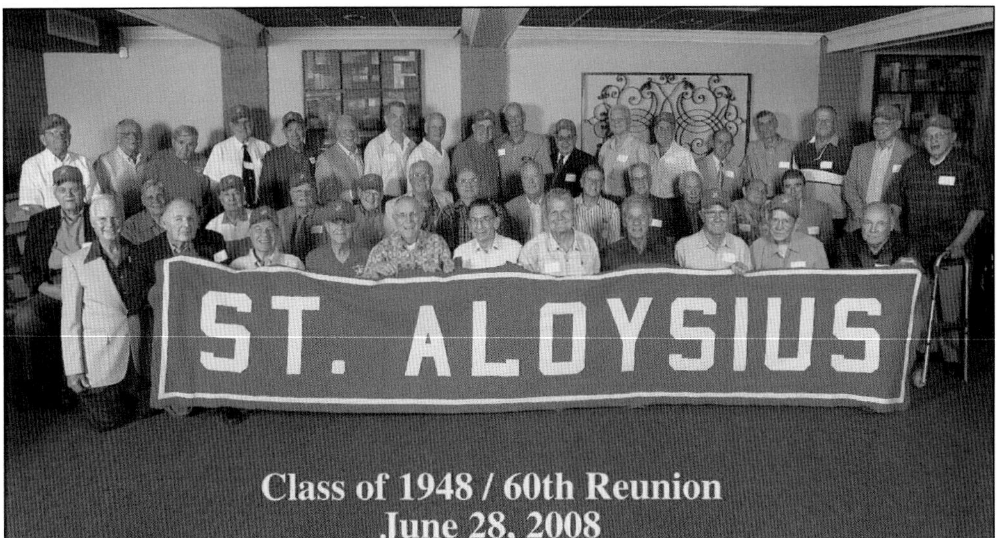

Sixty Years On . . . The 60-year reunion of the St. Aloysius class of 1948 was held on June 28, 2008. When asked to reminisce about their years on Esplanade Avenue and North Rampart Street, men who attended the school in the 1940s will often recall many positive experiences attending classes taught by the Brothers of the Sacred Heart.

Three

Expansion and Consolidation

"I have come to bring fire to the earth, and how I wish it were blazing already." (Lk 12:49)
This ardent desire of Jesus can only enkindle our hearts and excite our zeal. The love for our brothers and for the young people entrusted to us, then, radiates from Jesus' love for us. Our dedication to others, marked by respect, pardon, and unconditional love, will be a sign to them of the compassion of Christ.

—Article 118, *The Rule of Life of the Brothers of the Sacred Heart* (2007)

Brother Martinian's vision of a new BOSH school in the Gentilly Terrace neighborhood was brought to reality when Br. Martin Hernandez, SC, became provincial. Brother Martin's zeal (and considerable financial skills) enabled the province to put together the $1-million package needed to begin construction in Gentilly. Cor Jesu High School opened for the fall semester in 1954 with four freshmen classes, two sophomore classes, and a staff of seven Brothers. Cor Jesu earned accreditation in 1957 and graduated its first class that May (48 seniors). Athletic programs were slow to be implemented at Cor Jesu, giving the school an undeserved reputation as only being for intellectually elite students. Athletics came to the campus when a modern gymnasium was constructed under the guidance of principal Br. Gaspar Rodrigue, SC, in 1965. Enrollment took off as athletics grew at the school.

St. Aloysius continued to grow and prosper in the 1950s, but the campus was showing serious signs of age by the 1960s. The Brothers knew their mission in New Orleans would continue to expand and that Esplanade Avenue and North Rampart Street was not the best place for that expansion. By the end of the decade, the time had come to say good-bye to St. Aloysius and hello to a new future.

Leadership with Zeal! At prayer in the chapel are, from left to right, Brothers Warren Laudumiey (SA 1936), Finian Howe, Loyola Mattingly, Florent Favier, and Martin Hernandez, provincial of the U.S. province in the 1950s.

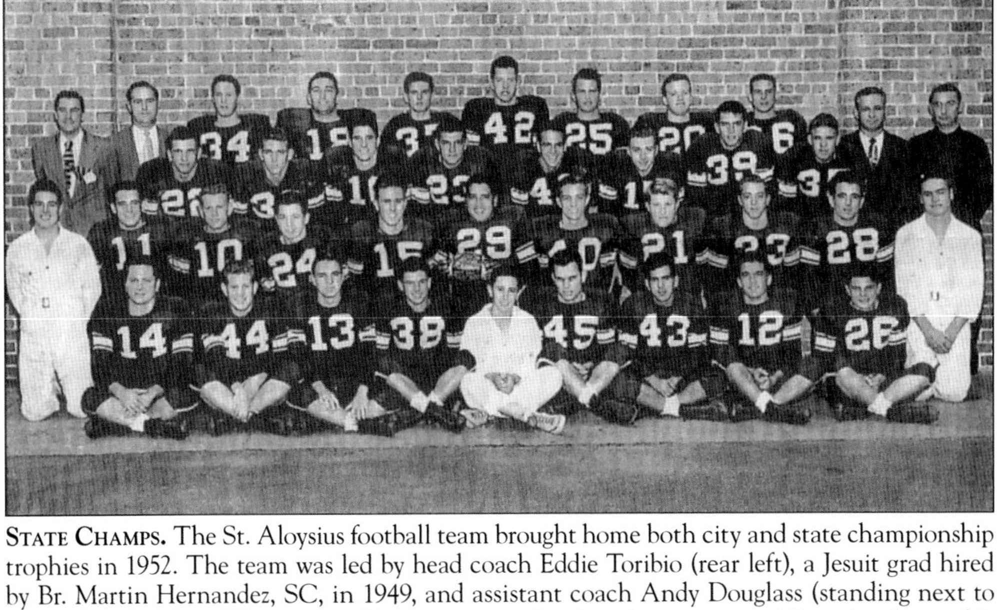

State Champs. The St. Aloysius football team brought home both city and state championship trophies in 1952. The team was led by head coach Eddie Toribio (rear left), a Jesuit grad hired by Br. Martin Hernandez, SC, in 1949, and assistant coach Andy Douglass (standing next to Toribio). After the 1952 victories, Toribio returned to his alma mater and Douglass began his 10-year tenure as head coach.

VIEW FROM ESPLANADE. This image is looking in through the front gate of St. Aloysius in the early 1950s.

RELAXATION. Enjoying some downtime on the D'Evereux Hall porch in Natchez, Mississippi, are, from left to right, Brothers Wilfrid Giral, Herman Boland, Will McCue, and Edgar Gagnon.

FINISHING TOUCHES. Landscapers and contractors work on the final phase of construction of Cor Jesu High in October 1954. The school opened on September 8 of that year. (Courtesy of the Historic New Orleans Collection.)

On Your Mark . . . Get Set . . . Go! Five members of the 1954 St. Aloysius track team pose for a photograph before a meet at Tad Gormley Stadium.

Gentilly Evening. Here is an after-dark shot of the main entrance of Cor Jesu High School.

CONTINUING EDUCATION. At left, attending a workshop in modern math held in 1960 at St. Stanislaus, are, from left to right, (first row) Brothers David Toups and More Schaefer; (second row) Brothers Roger Gaudin and Hubert Bonnette. Below, the same four Brothers (from left to right, Hubert, Roger, David, and More) are dressed more formally.

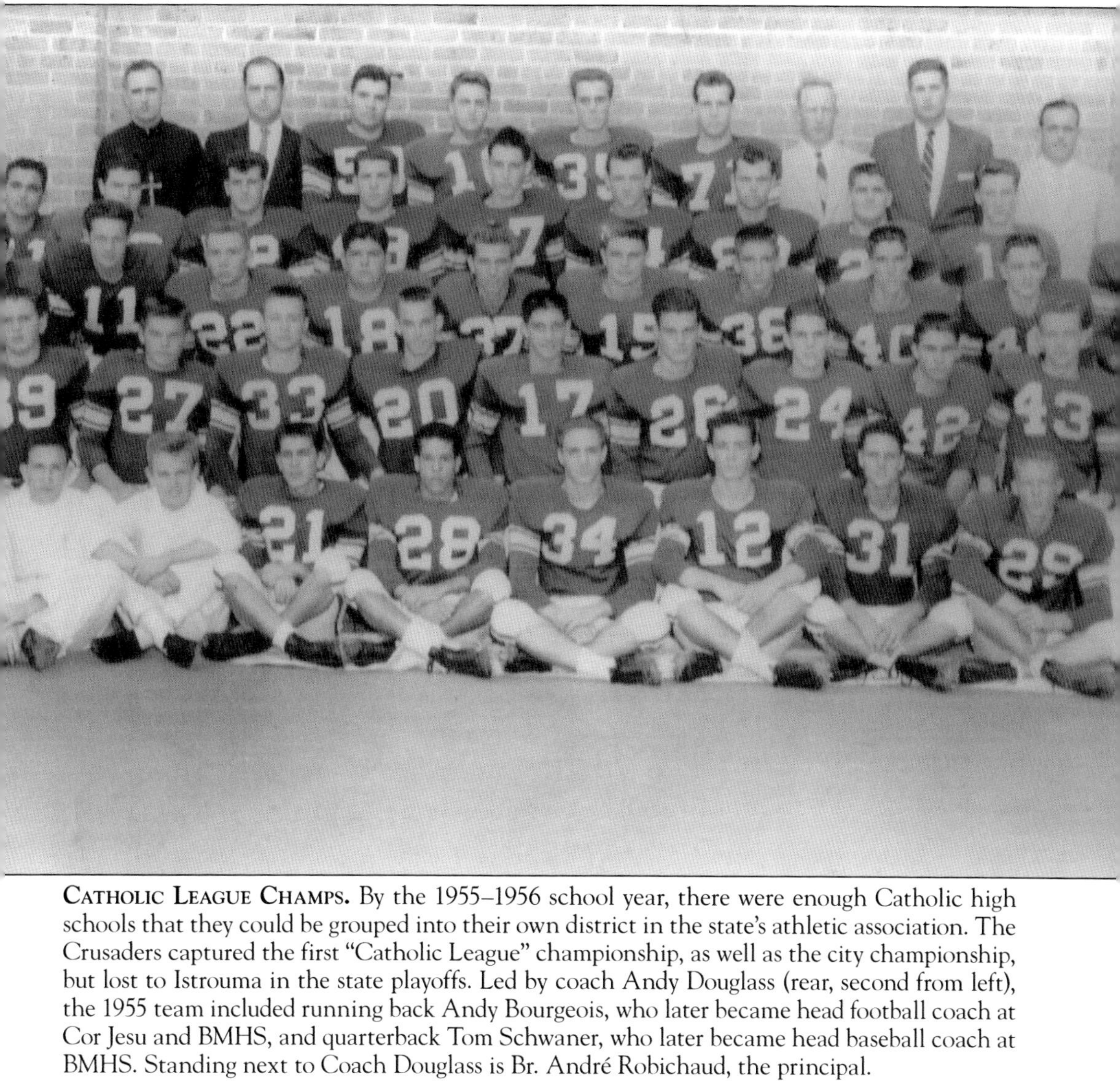

CATHOLIC LEAGUE CHAMPS. By the 1955–1956 school year, there were enough Catholic high schools that they could be grouped into their own district in the state's athletic association. The Crusaders captured the first "Catholic League" championship, as well as the city championship, but lost to Istrouma in the state playoffs. Led by coach Andy Douglass (rear, second from left), the 1955 team included running back Andy Bourgeois, who later became head football coach at Cor Jesu and BMHS, and quarterback Tom Schwaner, who later became head baseball coach at BMHS. Standing next to Coach Douglass is Br. André Robichaud, the principal.

Brothers' Residence. In addition to the new school in Gentilly, the New Orleans Province decided to construct a large residence facility on Elysian Fields Avenue. Located just north of the Cor Jesu High School building, the facility included both a chapel (right, behind the screen and statue) and the two-story residence.

In Training. William Engel (SA 1966) sprints to the finish of a practice run on the Esplanade Avenue neutral ground in 1965. Excelling as both a hurdler and a triple-jumper, Engel was the track team's MVP in 1965 and 1966. Engel was named BMHS Alumnus of the Year in 2007. (Courtesy of the *Clarion Herald*.)

LUNCH BREAK. Students hang out in the yard at St. Aloysius in 1965. St. Aloysuis students did not wear uniforms until the activation of the NJROTC unit for the 1967–1968 school year, and uniforms have continued through the BMHS years.

CHRISTMAS. A group of Brothers on the Cor Jesu faculty pose around the tree with Santa in this 1956 photograph: from left to right are Brothers Flavian Udinsky, Matthias Amos, Roger Gaudin, Lyn Bru, Elbert Farrelly, Celestine Algero, Donald Brady, Jerome Lepre, Alfred Rodriguez, and Florien McGinnis. The identity of Santa is unknown.

Postulants to Novices. Above, a group of young men at Sacred Heart Juniorate in Daphne, Alabama, begin their journey as Brothers of the Sacred Heart in 1962. Below are six of the same group of Postulants a year later, having just become novices in Belvedere, New Jersey. From left to right above are Brothers Raymond Sylve, Frank Boneno, John Auderer, Ronald Sylve (Raymond's twin), William Aucoin, David Pooley, and Xavier Werneth. The Sylve brothers joined the Brothers from St. Aloysius and Frank Boneno from Cor Jesu.

"The Greatest Bands in Dixie." The St. Aloysius Marching Band competes in the "battle of the bands" during the Krewe of Mid City Parade in 1969. The bands would stop in front of a reviewing stand at Canal Street and Jefferson Davis Parkway and perform for the judges.

ADMINISTRATIVE TEAM. Br. Remigius David, SC, president (left), and Br. Flavian Udinsky, SC, principal, were the last administrators at St. Aloysius.

QUIZZING CRUSADERS. These Crusaders represented St. Aloysius on the television show *Prep Quiz Bowl* in 1969. The game show for students was presented by WYES-TV, the first public television station in New Orleans.

CRUSADER BASEBALL, 1969. Glenn Masson (1971) heads toward home plate, followed by Steve Falati (SA 1969), on a grand slam hit by Gary Fraught (SA 1969) in the final baseball game against Cor Jesu.

Athletic Programs. From left to right, coaches Andy Bourgeois (SA 1956), Emile "Chubby" Marks (SA 1946), and Bob Conlin inspect the newly constructed locker room facilities at Cor Jesu. Bourgeois, who was head football coach at Cor Jesu and the first year of BMHS, was member of the legendary "Chinese Bandits" defense squad of LSU's National Championship team in 1958. (Courtesy of the *Clarion Herald*.)

Football. Coach Andy Bourgeois fits a Cor Jesu football player with a helmet in the school's library in 1968. (Courtesy of the *Clarion Herald*.)

ACADEMIC GAMES. At right, Crusaders Academic Gamers practice the competitive game Equations. Below are Br. Neal Golden (CJ 1957) and the Crusader Math Club.

Coach Conlin. Coach Bob Conlin is shown addressing a pep rally at Cor Jesu in 1967.

New Gym. The gymnasium at Cor Jesu is receiving some finishing touches before being dedicated and used for the 1966 school year. Cor Jesu did not have athletics when the school opened in 1954. The Brothers decided to build the gym and add athletics, fearing that the lack of sports programs was holding back enrollment at the school. The gym is still in use at BMHS. (Courtesy of the *Clarion Herald*.)

Vaudevillians. Br. Collin Dugas leads a group of Brothers in song at a St. Aloysius Mothers Club variety show.

CONLIN'S CREW. Coach Bob Conlin's first Cor Jesu basketball team is pictured in 1966.

COLOR GUARD. Prior to the activation of the school's NJROTC unit, the St. Aloysius Band also included a color guard for presenting the American flag at football games, Carnival parades, and other events.

One Hundred Years. This view is looking through the gate at the Esplanade Avenue side of St. Aloysius in 1969. To mark the 100th anniversary of the school, an electric sign was installed just above the main entrance.

House of Studies. Student Brothers are pictured in the recreation room of Sacred Heart Scholasticate in Mobile, Alabama, in the early 1960s.

Crusader Cheerleaders. The Crusader cheerleading squad was expanded to include girls for the first time in the 1964–1965 school year. Girls from all of the Catholic high schools in the city were invited to try out.

Cor Jesu. Shown here is a view of Cor Jesu from Elysian Fields Avenue. The modern view of BMHS from the same location is not all that much different; missing are a row of offices where the plants to the right of the entrance are and the classroom building and resource centers that were built behind the two-story building in this photograph.

Fall Afternoon. Two St. Aloysius students walk down Esplanade Avenue after class. They wear the uniforms of NJROTC cadets. The cadet on the left wears the regular, year-round uniform, while the young man on the right wears the fall/winter uniform (long-sleeved wool shirt and tie).

Brothers Who Were Brothers. They were both blood brothers and Brothers of the Sacred Heart, and they worked together. At left, Br. Cecil Hebert, SC, observes the batting technique of a Cor Jesu player. Below, Br. Edward Hebert watches as Cor Jesu football players scrimmage on the practice field behind the school. (Both courtesy of the *Clarion Herald*.)

NJROTC. For the 1967–1968 school year, students at St. Aloysius High became cadets in the Naval Junior Reserve Officers Training Corps. NJROTC cadets studied naval science in the classroom twice a week and marched outside during their weekly drill period. The unit was formally activated and commissioned on October 27, 1967, on the flight deck of the aircraft carrier USS *Lexington*, anchored at the Port of New Orleans. Above, one of the companies of the NJROTC battalion passes in review in the school's yard. At right, the drill team practices one of its parade maneuvers.

The 1966 Novices. The Novitiate class in 1966 was the first to keep their baptismal names when making their vows. They are, from left to right, (first row) Brothers Donald Delaune, New Orleans Province (NO), Roy O'Kiefe (NO), Thomas Feeney, New York Province (NY), and John Abate (NO) (SA 1965); (second row) Brothers William Cawley (NY), James Hackett (NY), Sam Clifford (NO) (SA 1965), Patrick McGinity (NO), Roy Wittendorffer (NO), Edward Deluzain (NO) (CJ 1965), and James Gallagher (NY); (third row) Brothers Melvin Estrade (NO) (SA 1965), William Frazier (NO), John Denniston (NY), Michael Phelan (NY), Carl Bouchereau (NO), and Timothy Casey (NO) (SA 1965). Brother Carl is currently a member of the BMHS Guidance Department.

Senior Status. A senior ring for the St. Aloysius class of 1969 is shown here. Senior rings are still an important status symbol in New Orleans culture.

Futbol. The 1969 Cor Jesu Soccer team was coached by Anthony Hartigan (top left).

Future Principal. Br. Mark Thornton, SC, reviews the design of the first BMHS senior ring with, from left to right, Neil Bero, Stan Stopa, and Bobby Taylor in 1969. These young men would become part of the charter class of BMHS the following year. Brother Mark became the combined school's first principal.

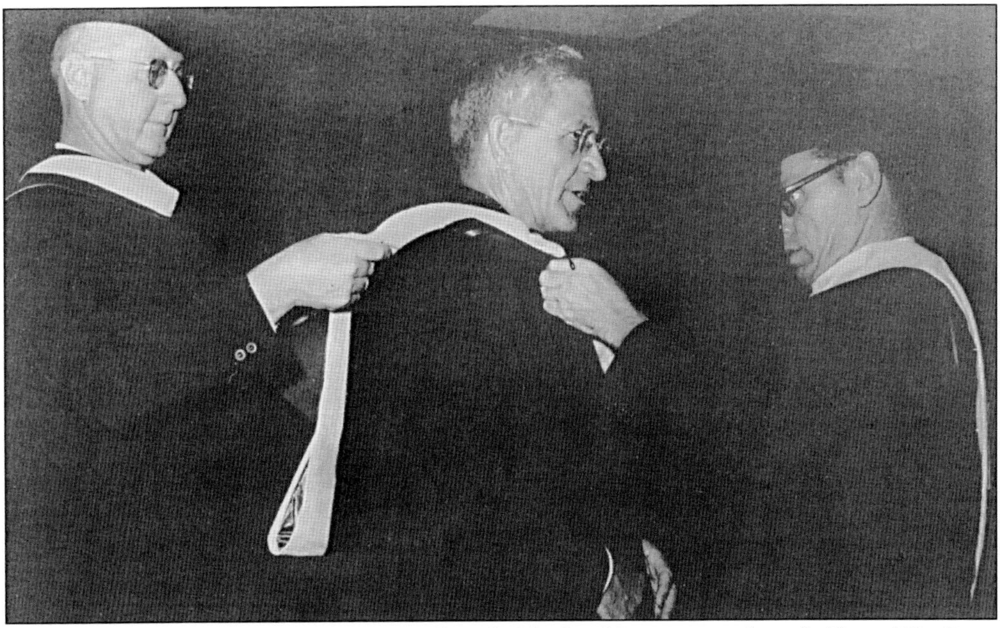

Pomp and Circumstance. Br. Remigius David, SC, St. Aloysius president (left), and Br. Rene LeBlanc, SC, (right) assist Br. Blaise Toups, SC, with his academic hood prior to the final commencement exercises for St. Aloysius High in 1969.

Graduation Mass. St. Frances Xavier Cabrini Church in Gentilly was the setting for the Commencement Mass of the Cor Jesu class of 1969. The neighborhood around Cabrini Church was inundated with 10 to 12 feet of water in the Flood of 2005. The church was demolished and is now the post-storm site of Holy Cross School.

Four

Unification

We adapt our apostolate of education to the needs of the time and place with clear-sightedness, good sense, and boldness in order to give the best possible response to the Spirit's calls.

—Article 150, *The Rule of Life of the Brothers of the Sacred Heart* (2007)

The Brothers were taking a huge risk in opening Brother Martin High School. Would the students accept the merger? How would former Cor Jesu students react to wearing uniforms and participating in NJROTC? Would alumni continue to support the institute by sending their sons and grandsons to the new school? The tensions grew so thick in October 1969 that the school's principal, Br. Mark Thornton, SC, had to return from the general chapter in Rome to sort things out. Brother Mark's administrative skills not only soothed the anxiety of students but were critical to managing a divided faculty of 80 (42 of whom were Brothers).

By decentralizing authority and decisions, Brother Mark managed to work out issues raised by faculty members. An undefeated basketball team winning the state championship that first year helped bring the student body together. Even though Brother Mark was elected provincial in the spring of 1970, his successor, Br. Brice Hendrick, SC, continued his policies. Both Brother Mark and Brother Brice made good use of Brothers who had the respect of alumni and parents, most notably Br. Nicholas Geisenberg, SC. "Brother Nick" was a stable presence in the classroom and at Parents' Club meetings. A second state basketball championship, followed by a football championship in the school's third year, brought teams and fans together. BMHS graduated the "First All-Martin Class" in 1973, young men who attended BMHS from freshmen to senior year. From that point on, there were no longer Aloysius or Cor Jesu boys in classes; unification was complete.

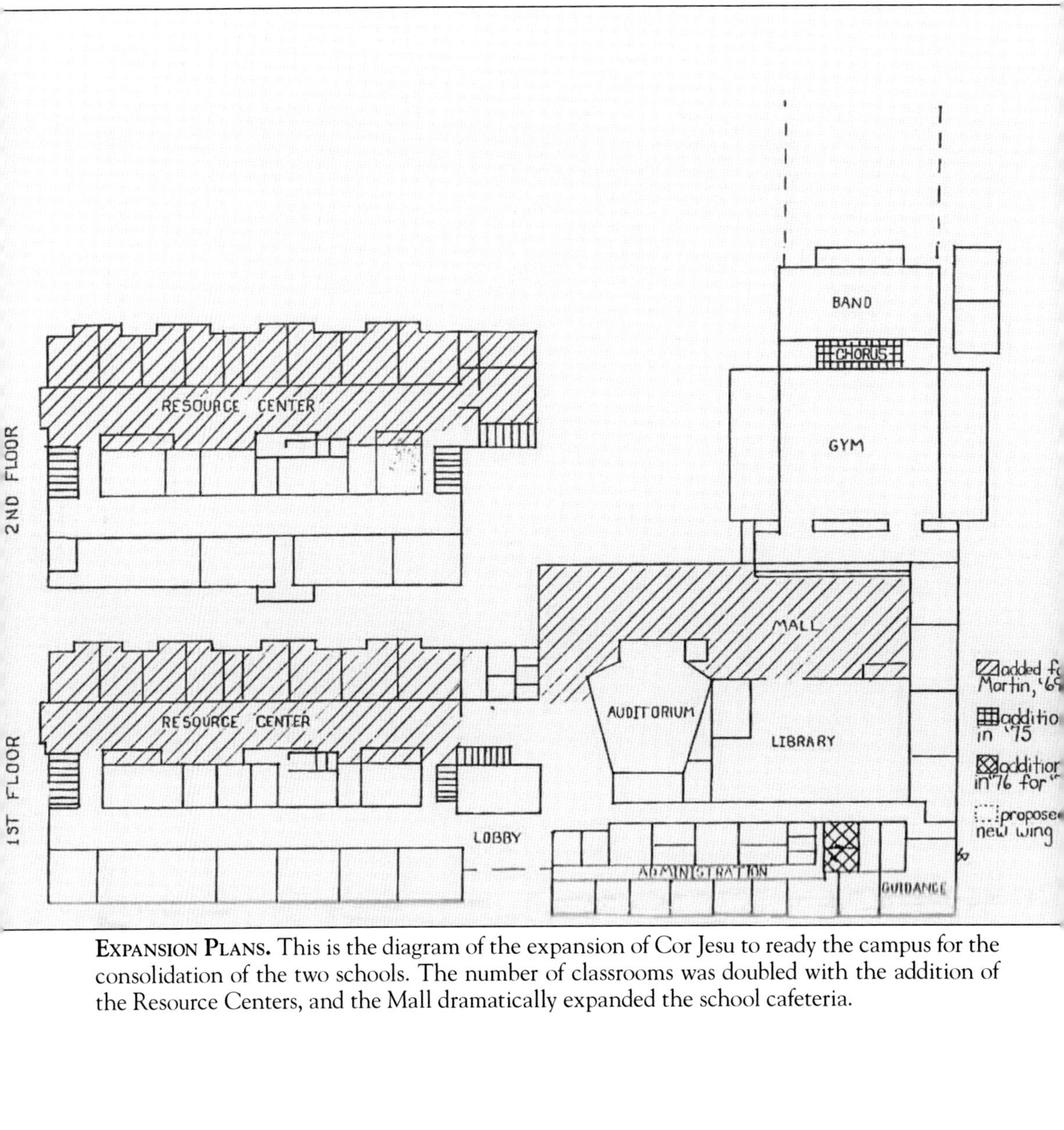

Expansion Plans. This is the diagram of the expansion of Cor Jesu to ready the campus for the consolidation of the two schools. The number of classrooms was doubled with the addition of the Resource Centers, and the Mall dramatically expanded the school cafeteria.

THE MALL. The expansion of the cafeteria at Cor Jesu became the most visible (and most used) component of Brother Martin High. The Mall was more than just a lunchroom; meetings, Parents' Club functions, and even school dances were held in this multipurpose facility. Here a group of students enjoys some free time in 1979.

CRAB BOIL. A group of Brothers is enjoying two New Orleans classics—boiled seafood and beer—in 1971.

BY THE BAY. From left to right, Brothers Alcuin Kelly, Donald McGrath, Nicholas Geisenberg, and Lloyd LeBlanc pose for a photograph at St. Stanislaus in the 1970s.

BMHS BAND. Unifying St. Aloysius and Cor Jesu under a new name presented a challenge for the school's band. There were no uniforms for the combined school, so the marching band wore their NJROTC service dress blue uniforms when performing. Above, the band poses for a portrait in 1969. Below is the band in the stands at Tad Gormley Stadium for a football game.

Personal Attention. Br. Brice Hendrick, SC, works to resolve a student's scheduling conflict. Brother Brice became BMHS's second principal when Br. Mark Thorton, SC, became provincial in May 1970.

Coaching Staff. Head football coach Bob Conlin (center) is flanked by his brother Dan (left) and Emile "Chubby" Marks (right) in 1973. (Courtesy of the *Clarion Herald*.)

Resource Centers. To connect the original Cor Jesu classroom building with the expansion wing behind it, a large corridor was constructed. This area was carpeted and designated as Resource Centers (upstairs and downstairs). Students could study individually, meet with teachers, or work in small groups in these areas. Above, Br. Jerome Lepre, SC, (standing) confers with Br. Henry Gaither, SC, in the downstairs Resource Center. Below, a student catches up on assigned reading while sitting in a carrel.

Serenading Students. Led by Br. Virgil Harris, SC, the BMHS Concert Band is shown in 1971 performing for students in the gym.

Not Just Football and Basketball. The 1971 State Championship cross-country team is pictured here. Combining the talent of two of the top schools in the city was a significant factor in the early success of BMHS athletic teams. Coach Jack Schommer's successful St. Aloysius running program carried over to Gentilly and continues to this day.

Registration. BMHS used a college-style system for class registration. Assisting students with the process at the start of the 1972–1973 school year are, from left to right, Brothers David Toups, SC; Maurus Bordelon, SC (SA 1955); and Ivy LeBlanc, SC. Seated next to Brother Ivy is Don Bagert (1973).

Hustle-Bustle. The usually quiet Resource Center is full of activity between classes in 1971. Br. Jay Faust, SC, is just visible to the right making his way to the faculty lounge.

Band Programs. In addition to the marching and concert bands, the BMHS music staff also encouraged and assisted with smaller combo bands. At left, Keith Keller, band director (left, with clarinet); Michael Cottingham, chorus director (center, with baton); and Arthur Hardy (right, with trombone) pose with students in 1973. Below, Keller and Hardy pose with their summer band students for 1973. They are standing at the entrance of the old band room, which has since been torn down and replaced by the Ridgely Fine Arts Center.

Regimental Reviews. The NJROTC unit grew from battalion size at St. Aloysius to a regiment of ten 100-cadet companies at BMHS, since all upperclassmen (10th through 12th graders) were required to participate in the program. Above, from left to right, Br. Brice Hendrick, SC; Adm. Elmo Zumwalt, chief of naval operations; and Comdr. George Kelly, U.S. Navy (Retired), stand as the regiment passes in review. (Br. Martin Hernandez, SC, is seated in the rear, wearing a cowboy hat.) Below, the NJROTC Drill Team performs a routine for the VIPs.

Third Principal. At left, Br. Donnan Berry, SC, (SA 1944) became the third BMHS principal in the 1975–1976 school year. He was assisted by the other men in the sketches below: Br. Ivy LeBlanc, SC, (top right) vice principal–discipline; and Louis Levy (bottom), vice principal–academics. The sketches were drawn by William McGreal (1976).

CARNIVAL TIME. Br. Leo Godin, SC, chats with students while waiting for a Mardi Gras Parade in 1973.

EXPANSION PLANS. From left to right, Norman Prendergast; Br. Lee Barker, SC, provincial; Br. Donnan Berry, SC, (SA 1944) BMHS principal; Bishop Stanley Ott (SA 1944), auxiliary bishop of New Orleans; and Tom Gilmore (SA 1940) review plans for expanding the campus with an addition to the north end of the second-floor Resource Center. That addition was constructed but then demolished to make way for the Meyer Math and Science Center, opened in 2008.

IBM Selectrics. Br. Lloyd LeBlanc, SC, supervises a typing class in 1979. The development of personal computers would soon overshadow the IBM typewriters in use at this time.

Third Championship. Coach Tom Kolb and the 1973–1974 basketball team are pictured moments after winning the final game of the state tournament in Alexandria. The team was led on the court by senior Rick Robey (no. 53, just to the right of the trophy), who went on to win championships with the University of Kentucky and the NBA's Boston Celtics.

Uniform Evolution. Anticipating the curriculum change making NJROTC an option for students in 1975–1976, the band purchased new uniforms the year before. At right are band officers from 1970 in their navy uniforms. Below, in 1978, drum major Kurt Engelhardt is pictured in the band's first non-navy uniform. (Engelhardt is now a federal judge in New Orleans.)

Brother Jean. In his roles as director of student activities, director of development, and assistant to the president, no one person represented the charism of the Brothers of the Sacred Heart to the public more than Br. Jean Sobert, SC. Brother Jean is seen here displaying a teacher appreciation gift.

The View from Elysian Fields Avenue. Motorists driving past BMHS in the 1970s would notice little change in the school from Cor Jesu High in the 1960s. Other than the redesign of the sign, the look was essentially the same. The major changes and expansion of the school took place behind the "old" building.

LIBRARY SCIENCE. Above, members of the Library Club often manned the desk in the school library, enabling the librarians to do other work or grab some lunch.

RENEWAL. Br. Francis David, SC, is shown renewing his vows in the St. Stanislaus chapel in 1975. The celebrant (in white) is Br. William McCue, SC. Brother Francis was a teacher and assistant principal at BMHS in the 1970s and 1980s.

SCHOOL'S OUT! Students have some after-class downtime while waiting for rides in October 1973.

SEAFOOD DINNER. Enjoying themselves at an alumni function are Br. Jean Sobert, SC (center), Br. Bernard Couvillion, SC (left, with back to camera), and Br. Thomas Duggar, SC (right).

Freshman Initiation. Seniors "anoint" freshmen with crimson (ketchup) and gold (mustard) during initiation activities in the fall of 1972.

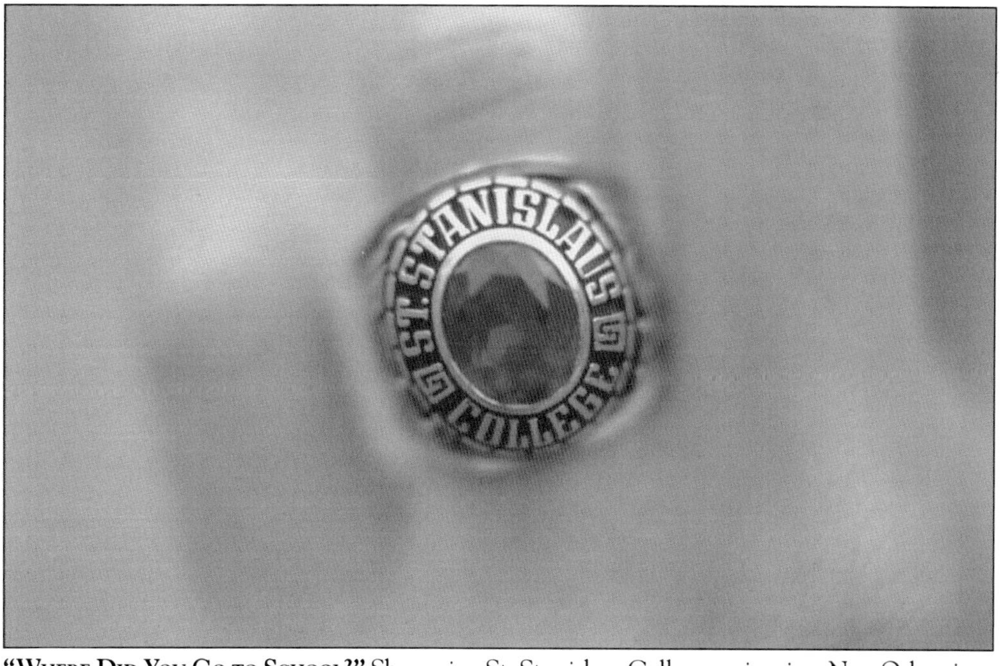

"Where Did You Go to School?" Shown is a St. Stanislaus College senior ring. New Orleanians care more about where someone went to high school than any college/university/graduate work one might do later in life. Senior rings are one of the easiest ways that "Brothers Boys" can identify each other.

EXCELLENCE CUT SHORT. Br. More Schaefer, SC, taught math at BMHS in the 1970s and 1980s, but his career was cut too short with his passing in 1983 at the age of 50. Above, Brother More lectures to calculus students. (The author is proud to have been one of the "celebrated reprobates of third period Calculus" in 1975–1976.) Below, Brother More's role as moderator of the tennis team is illustrated. An annual Brother More Schaefer Award is presented to the teacher of the year at BMHS.

Five

CENTURY II

It is an apostolic necessity that we stay well informed of the latest developments in the field of education and of the teaching of the Church on social problems.

—Article 151, *The Rule of Life of the Brothers of the Sacred Heart* (2007)

Twenty-five years after the Brothers opened their second school in New Orleans, and 10 years after consolidating those schools into one, the institute moved forward in its second century of service in the United States. Academically, the 1980s were a time for evaluating the innovations and changes of the 1970s, keeping what worked, discarding what did not, and returning to traditional forms of instruction where appropriate. Computers came to the classrooms, but Brothers were leaving. Even though the cold war was coming to a close in the 1980s, the institute had to address many of the societal changes around them. For example, Br. Xavier Werneth, SC, during his term as provincial (1982–1988), supervised committees working on projects as diverse as an educational mission statement, organization of ordained brothers, vocational development, spiritual life, and formation of effective policies addressing HIV/AIDS.

In 1994, Br. Ronald Talbot, SC, left his position as principal at E. D. White in Houma, marking the first time that all principals of BOSH schools in the province were lay colleagues. Br. Bernard Couvillion, SC, provincial at that time, recognized the need to begin restructuring the business side of BOSH schools, incorporating them and establishing various foundations to continue the work of the institute into the future.

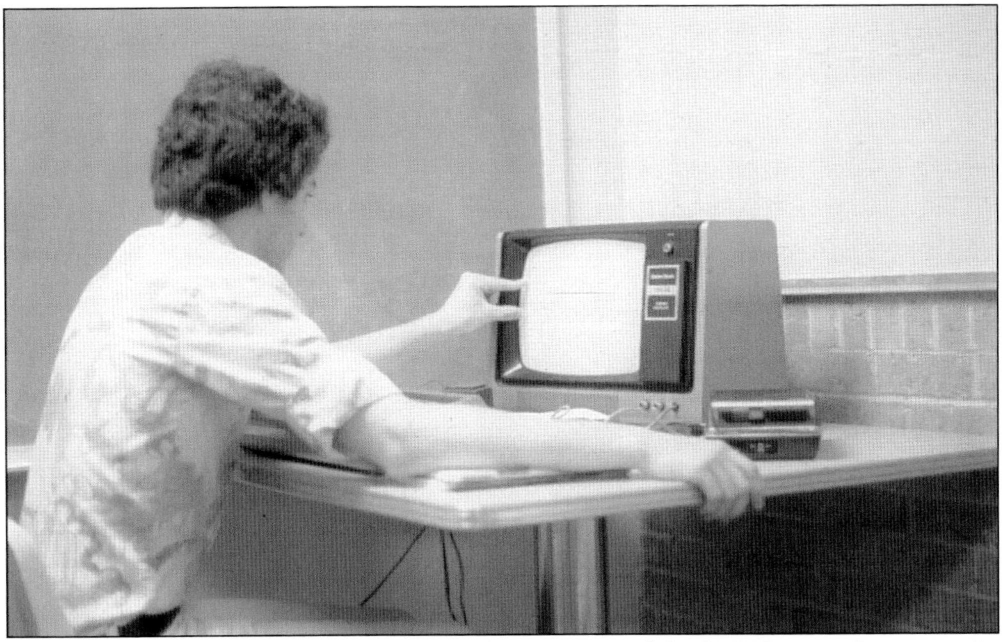

Personal Computers. Computer science had been a part of the BMHS curriculum since the beginning. Br. Flavian Udinsky, SC, tasked Br. Neal Golden, SC, with developing a computer science class in the 1960s at St. Aloysius. By the 1980s, the school switched from timesharing access to PCs, starting with the TRS-80 Model I, as shown here.

Gridiron Mentors. Head football coach Bob Conlin and his 1985 staff are pictured here. From left to right are (kneeling) coaches Elmore Steinart, Nick Lagatutta (1971), Barry Hebert (1974), Emile Fair (1971), and Emile "Chubby" Marks (SA 1954); (standing) coaches Don Klos, Ray Charbonneau, Conlin, A. J. Musso, and Mike Materne (1971).

LEGION CHAMPS. The BMHS 1983 American Legion baseball team is pictured here. Legion teams play during the summer break and are sponsored by local businesses. This year, the Wendy's-sponsored Crusader team won the state championship. This photograph was taken at the Legion World Series tournament in Fargo, North Dakota, where the Crusaders won third place. The team, under the direction of coach Barry Hebert (1973), would go on to win the regular-season state championship the following year.

CHALLENGING STUDENTS. Br. Bernard Couvillion, SC, leads a literature discussion in one of his English classes.

GENTILLY EXCELLENCE. Br. Ivy LeBlanc, SC, principal (left), and John Devlin, assistant principal, display the "Excellence in Education" banner the school received.

VAMOS! Soccer returned to Elysian Fields Avenue in the 1980s, having taken a hiatus since Cor Jesu's 1969 team (see page 73). This is the 1983 team.

ST. ANNE'S. Br. John Hoststream, SC, spends time with a young man at St. Anne's Navajo Mission in Klagetoh, Arizona.

Intramurals. Beginning in the 1970s, the BMHS intramurals program grew into a very successful part of student life. Here a football team composed of band members poses outside the old band room in the mid-1980s.

Assembly. In 1988, the New Orleans Province named then-principal Br. Ivy LeBlanc, SC, to be the school's first president, and John Devlin became the first lay principal in BMHS history. Here Devlin addresses a student assembly.

"Mardi Hardy." Arthur Hardy was the director of the BMHS band for 10 years. In 1977, he published the first edition of *Arthur Hardy's Mardi Gras Guide*, an annual magazine that includes parade schedules, route maps, Krewe history, and other interesting Carnival facts. Above, Hardy is pictured with the Crusader Marching Band on a parade route. At right is the cover of the 1988 issue of the *Guide*. (Right courtesy of Arthur Hardy.)

"Brother Nick." Br. Nicholas Geisenberg, SC, was a beloved teacher of generations of St. Aloysius, Cor Jesu, and BMHS students. In addition to teaching math, Brother Nicholas served as assistant principal at Cor Jesu in 1969. After retiring from the classroom, Brother Nicholas remained active on campus, managing the school's bookstore and as a dedicated fan of BMHS sports, particularly baseball. Above, Brother Nicholas is on duty in the bookstore in the late 1990s. Below, the BMHS baseball team honored Brother Nicholas by asking him to throw out the first pitch of the final game of the 2003 season. (Below courtesy of Danny Ford, father of Jeremy [2003] and Braeden [2009].)

Quiz Bowlers. BMHS continued to participate in the televised Quiz Bowl competition throughout the 1980s and 1990s, until the show was cancelled for lack of sponsorship. The Quiz Bowl teams now compete in non-televised local and state tournaments. Here Ricky Nusselein (left) and show moderator Dan Milham (right), WDSU-TV's meteorologist, pose with a team from the early 1990s.

MS-DOS. Computer labs at BMHS moved to IBM-compatible systems by the early 1990s. The State of Louisiana required that all freshmen take a half-semester computer literacy course, so the BMHS computer science department expanded from a couple of high-level classes for seniors to include these literacy classes.

Hospitality Center. In 1990, the province sold its two houses at 1920 and 1930 Robert E. Lee Boulevard and purchased the church building across the street from BMHS at 4600 Elysian Fields Avenue. The building had most recently housed a Lutheran congregation. The Brothers renovated the facility, using it as a hospitality center. Young men discerning vocations could live at the center temporarily to experience community life.

Barbershop. From left to right, Brothers Paul Montero (teacher and assistant principal of St. Aloysius in the 1960s), Adrian Gaudin, Donnan Berry (SA 1944), and Pierre St. Pierre sing barbershop-quartet style in the St. Stanislaus College school resource center in 1994.

From 1869 to 1994. The year 1994 marked the 125th year of BOSH schools in New Orleans. To mark the anniversary, the main entrance was renovated to create "Place Sacre Coeur." Brothers who served as president and/or principal at one of the three schools gathered to celebrate. They are, from left to right, Brothers Donnan Berry (SA 1944), Lee Barker, Ivy LeBlanc, Flavian Udinsky, Gaspar Rodrigue, Felician Fourrier, Mark Thornton, and Remigius David.

Laity in Charge. Gene Tullier was BMHS's second lay principal. Tullier, whose career at BMHS began in 1978, served BMHS as a teacher, department chairman, assistant principal, and vice principal. In 1999, Br. Ivy LeBlanc, SC, was elected provincial, Principal John Devlin took over as BMHS president, and Tullier became principal.

St. Aloysius, 1944. From left to right, Br. Ivy LeBlanc, SC; Tom Benson (SA 1944); and Br. Jean Sobert, SC, inspect progress on the construction of the St. Aloysius Class of 1944 Gymnasium, located in the Ridgley Center. Benson, the owner of the NFL's Super Bowl Champion New Orleans Saints, was instrumental in leading the fund-raising campaign to finance the gym, which is dedicated to his graduating class.

THE ALOYSIUS COLUMN. Concerned that the last remaining brick column from the fence surrounding the St. Aloysius campus on Esplanade Avenue and North Rampart Street would be destroyed, a group of Aloysius alumni from classes in the 1950s donated time and money to relocate the column to BMHS in 1994 (above). At right, the column now stands in front of the Ridgley Center.

THE RIDGLEY CENTER. A major expansion program came to fruition in January 1999 with the dedication of the Thomas F. and Elaine P. Ridgley Fine Arts and Athletic Center. Thomas Ridgley is a 1951 graduate of St. Aloysius. The band and chorus rooms behind the BMHS gymnasium were demolished, and a two-story facility containing an auxiliary gym, band room, chorus room, fine arts and general classrooms, and offices was constructed. Above is the Ridgley Center. Below, Br. Nicholas Geisenberg, SC (first row, fourth from the right), poses with the Cor Jesu alumni present at the building's dedication ceremony.

DEDICATED SERVICE. Brothers celebrating jubilees at St. Stanislaus in 2002 are, from left to right, Warren Laudumiey (SA 1936) (65th), Celestine Algero (50th), Matthias Amos (50th), and Ray Kuhn (25th).

PLANNING FOR THE FUTURE. Members of the BMHS Foundation's Institutional Development Team posing for a photograph at the annual Alumnus of the Year Mass in 2005 are, from left to right, John Devlin, BMHS president; Jeanette Bovenzi; Ashley Lensmeyer; Tommy Mitchell (1979), assistant to the president and director of development; Kenny Spellman (1984), alumni director; Gabrielle Macaluso, assistant principal for admissions; Julia Gandolfi, community relations director; Br. Jean Sobert, SC, assistant to the president; and Sr. Joan LaPlace, CSJ. (Positions mentioned here are the current jobs committee members hold.)

Seven Principals. At the reception following Br. David Landry's vow ceremony on July 28, 2002, Susan Estrade took a rare moment to gather with seven St. Stanislaus principals under whom she has served, including, from left to right, Brothers Celestine Algero, Paul Montero, Eldon Crifasi, Ronald Talbot (current provincial), Lee Barker, Ronald Hingle (1978) (current SSC principal), and Paul Mulligan. Estrade joined the SSC faculty in 1972 and currently is academic assistant principal.

Group Discussion. Chatting at a workshop at the BOSH Hospitality Center on Elysian Fields Avenue in 2004 are, from left to right, Br. Francis David, SC; Br. Ivy LeBlanc, SC; Greg Brandao, assistant principal at BMHS in the 1990s; and Br. Xavier Werneth, SC.

Farley Field. Prior to its acquisition by the New Orleans Province, the land bordering Gentilly Boulevard, Mandeville Street, Stephen Girard Drive, and Marigny Street was the E. A. Farley Florist shop and nursery. Above, Mrs. Farley and Gene Tullier, principal, unveil the sign in front of E. A. Farley Field in September 1999. Below, Br. Louis Couvillon, SC, one of the institute's ordained brothers and BMHS chaplain, blesses representatives of the band, NJROTC, and the various athletic teams who would use the Farley Field facilities.

COINDRE LEADERSHIP. Preparing for a new millennium where the number of men taking the habit will be much, much smaller is a challenge the Brothers of the Sacred Heart are meeting head on. The institute created the Coindre Leadership Program, an intense personal formation program to help participants to understand the educational charism of the institute. The "charism" of a religious congregation is that certain spiritual something that makes the congregation unique. The Coindre Leadership Program pairs lay men and women working in BOSH schools with Brothers as mentors. The participants make use of directed readings, essential experiences, and BOSH communal experiences to help them grow in the charism. Above, Brothers of the New Orleans Province induct John Devlin (president, BMHS, at left) and Dr. Greg Brandao (development director, Catholic High) into the program in 2003.

Six

Phoenix Rising

Christian education cannot easily be realized without the witness of a school community which is built on close relationships among teachers, parents, students, and the local people. We wholeheartedly support the establishment of programs for participation and animation which give dynamism to the school community, especially through the search for a common educational vision.

—Article 156, *The Rule of Life of the Brothers of the Sacred Heart* (2007)

On the evening of Thursday, August 25, 2005, the BMHS class of 2006 gathered with family and friends at St. Joseph's Church on Tulane Avenue to celebrate their Ring Mass and receive their class rings. Four days later, the world changed for all New Orleanians with the landfall of Hurricane Katrina and the subsequent failure of man-made levees and floodwalls. While the damage to the BMHS campus was relatively light compared to the rest of the Gentilly neighborhood, the metro area overall was such a mess that hundreds of thousands of people were unable to return home for several weeks. Led by Nick Lagatutta (1971), facilities director, and John Devlin, BMHS president, teams of faculty/staff, alumni, and volunteers descended on the campus to begin the process of rebuilding.

The New Orleans Province, in consultation with its lay colleagues, made the decision to restructure the school day at Catholic High in Baton Rouge, Louisiana, to allow the BMHS staff to conduct classes in the evenings. Catholic High's school day would start earlier than normal, and the campus would be turned over to BMHS in the late afternoon. Brother Martin/Baton Rouge opened on September 12, 2005. The school accepted both boys and girls from Catholic schools in New Orleans. Some students attended classes at Archbishop Rummel and Archbishop Chapelle in Metairie; some remained farther away from the metro area, in Houston, Memphis, or Atlanta. Sadly, some families and students never returned after the storm.

The hard work of the teams at BMHS paid off; the school was ready to reopen in January 2006. The boys returned for the spring semester, salvaging at least half of the year. Like so many in the metro area, the BMHS community continues to rebuild and return to what was considered "normal" pre-storm. BMHS rises from the flood, a phoenix spreading its wings to soar to new heights.

THE BRICK. At the beginning of the 2006–2007 school year, a brick was removed from the wall of the original Cor Jesu classroom building and presented by the BMHS community to Catholic High in Baton Rouge. A plaque was placed above the space in the wall, which reads as follows: "The brick removed from this space at the front entrance of our school was presented to the students and faculty of Catholic High School on Monday, December 19, 2005 to commemorate their generosity in sharing their Baton Rouge campus with us for three months after Hurricane Katrina. We will never forget this outstanding demonstration of compassion in the spirit of the Brothers of the Sacred Heart."

BMHS/BR Band. The show went on, in spite of the inability of the BMHS band directors to be in Baton Rouge in the fall of 2005. Drum major Mark Messina (2006) conducts the 45-man Crusader Band at one of only three football games of the 2005 season, versus Archbishop Rummel High at ARHS in Metairie. (Courtesy of Jack Dever, father of John [2010].)

Returning to Normal. The BMHS campus began to show more and more signs of normalcy as the spring semester of 2006 drew to a close. Here, from left to right, QMC Terry Necaise, U.S. Navy (Retired); Maj. Lester Amick, U.S. Marine Corps (Retired); and Gene Tullier present awards to the NJROTC cadets in each class (freshman through senior) who had the highest academic averages.

Leadership Change. In May 2006, Gene Tullier was named president of Catholic High School in Baton Rouge, Louisiana. Greg Rando (1977), BMHS's vice principal, became principal in Gentilly. Above is Rando addressing a group of sixth- and seventh-graders considering BMHS in the school's auditorium at "Crusader Discovery Night." Below, from left to right, Justin Fleetwood, assistant principal for discipline; Tom Mavor, vice principal for academics; and Rando enjoy a night out with the faculty at Ye Olde College Inn.

GOOD SAMARITANS. Students and Marianist Brothers from Chaminade High in Mineola, New York, visit BMHS and New Orleans in February 2009. The Chaminade community provided much-needed assistance to BMHS after the storm, raising funds to put together backpacks equipped with school supplies for each student at Brother Martin/Baton Rouge.

VOCATIONS. Br. Chris Sweeney, SC, speaks to students about the institute at the school's annual Career Day in the fall of 2009.

Looking up Elysian Fields Avenue. New landscaping makes it difficult to see the school's main entrance from the corner (compare with pages 68 and 93). A new formal sign, visible on the right, was erected at the corner of Elysian Fields Avenue and St. Aloysius Drive in 2007.

Campus Expansion. The Roland H. and Macy Paton Meyer Science and Mathematics Building was dedicated on November 10, 2007. Roland Meyer is a 1945 graduate of St. Aloysius. The Meyer Building stands on the site of the old Brothers' Residence (page 56), built north of the original Cor Jesu building.

School Liturgy. The only place on campus large enough to hold the entire BMHS community for mass is the Conlin Gym. Above, Br. Louis Couvillon, SC, celebrates the Eucharist, with the band behind him and faculty and students sitting in the bleachers. Below, Melanie Williams conducts the BMHS Chorus at mass.

SUMMER STAR. D. J. Augustin (2006), center, relaxes with boys attending his summer basketball camp in July 2009. In his freshman year, the Crusaders were state runners-up in basketball; Augustin led the team to state championships in his sophomore and junior years. He now plays for the Charlotte Bobcats of the NBA.

SNOW! This snow day on December 11, 2008, was the first in over 10 years at BMHS. Though there was not enough white stuff to justify closing school, students did get a chance to get out and throw snowballs for a while in the morning.

RECRUITING. The downsizing of Metro New Orleans' population in the wake of the storm makes the BMHS community keenly aware of the importance of recruiting new students. Above, members of the Academic Games team man a table at "Crusader Discovery Night," an open house–style event designed to introduce prospective students to the wide variety of extracurricular programs available. Below, two Crusader cheerleaders pose with a group of youngsters touring the school.

CajunFest. Above is a view of the parking lot across the street from the school, converted into a fair site for a weekend each spring.

Field Trip. One of Justin Fleetwood's sophomore English classes is seen here visiting Chalmette National Battlefield in the spring of 2009.

The Great Read. Each summer, the BMHS faculty selects a book as required summer reading for all students. Parents and other family members are encouraged to join their sons in "The Great Read." The book for 2008, *Ghost Soldiers*, a World War II book by Hampton Sides, was so popular that Sides was asked to speak to the school. Above, the NJROTC Color Guard presents the colors at the beginning of the assembly. Below, from left to right, Maj. Lester Amick, Cadet Commander Gregory Gaumond, Sides, Cadet Lieutenant Paul Wood, and Chief Necaise pause for a photograph after Sides's presentation.

Alumni Events. Above, from left to right, Thomas Ridgley (SA 1951), his wife, Elaine, and Br. Ivy LeBlanc, SC, are pictured at the annual Prayer Breakfast.

Red Mass. The BMHS Chorus sang for the annual "Red Mass" on October 5, 2009. Joining the chorus in the photograph is the Most Reverend Gregory M. Aymond (CJ 1967), archbishop of New Orleans.

Jazzy Morning. Dominick Caronna (1985) conducts the jazz band before school in January 2009.

Changing Sports Scene. The roller hockey team is shown in action in the 2008 season. Roller hockey competition is currently at the club level; players, parents, and coaches are working to have the sport endorsed by the Louisiana High School Athletic Association (LHSAA).

Dwindling Numbers. Four of the five Brothers working at BMHS for the 2009–2010 school year join at the Founder's Day Liturgy on September 30, 2009. Br. Louis Couvillon, SC, is the celebrant. Behind him are, from left to right, Brothers Neal Golden, Carl Boucheron, and Chris Sweeney. Br. Teri Falgout is not pictured.

Halftime. The BMHS Crusader Marching Band performs at a football game at Ted Gormley Stadium. The young ladies pictured are members of the "Debs" from St. Mary's Dominican High School in New Orleans. Instead of having a school-sponsored dance team, BMHS joins up with Dominican for football season and the annual Marching Festival competition.

Future Generations. Members of the BMHS faculty who are also BOSH alumni gather after the Founder's Day Liturgy on September 30, 2009. Touched by the charism of the institute in their formative years, these men continue to grow in the traditions and philosophy of the Brothers, passing on the charism to future generations of students. Even if there would come that very sad day when the Brothers are no longer, men like these would keep the charism alive in the hearts and spirits of the young people they teach. The Brothers of the Sacred Heart and BMHS are online at brothersofthesacredheart.org and brothermartin.com.

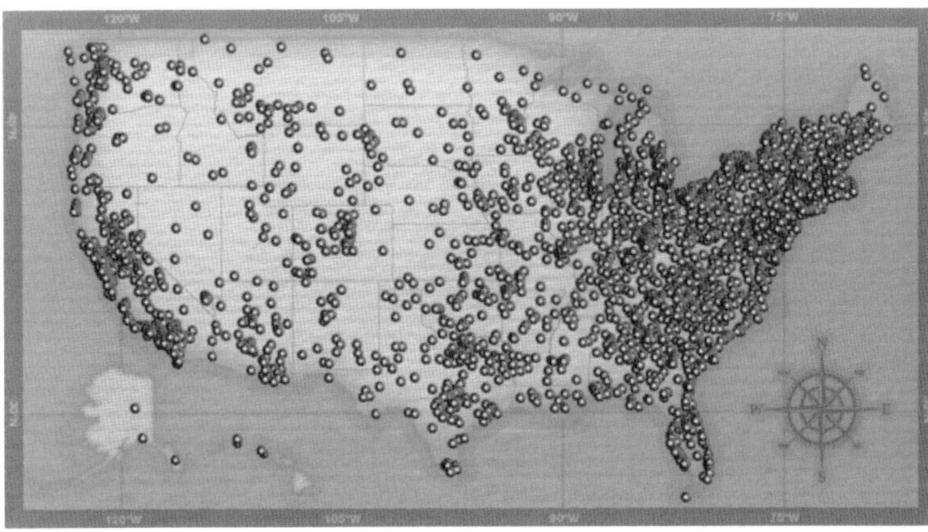